WHEN YOU NEED A
Little Hug

ARTWORK BY TERESA KOGUT

HARVEST HOUSE PUBLISHERS

EUGENE, OREGON

How Beautiful a day can be when friendship touches it

WHEN YOU NEED A LITTLE HUG

Text Copyright © 2005 by Harvest House Publishers
Eugene, Oregon 97402

ISBN-10: 0-7369-1623-7
ISBN-13: 978-0-7369-1623-3

The Linda McDonald Agency
5200 Park Rd, Suite 104
Charlotte, NC 28209
(704) 370-0057

Design and production by Koechel Peterson & Associates, Inc., Minneapolis, Minnesota

TO _____

WITH LOVE _____

Once upon a time, in a warm little corner of my heart,

there lived a very special little hug.

It was a very special little hug simply because

it was being saved for a certain moment

when it would be needed most

by someone who meant the world to me.

I'm sending that very special little hug to you today

because it seemed like just the right time,

and because you are someone

who does mean the world to me.

_____

Author Unknown

IT TAKES A LONG TIME TO
GROW AN OLD FRIEND

A FRIEND ALWAYS KNOWS WHEN YOU NEED A HUG.

A true friend warms you
by her presence, trusts you with her secrets,
and remembers you in her prayers.

WHEN THE NEWS IS ALL BAD

AND THE SKY IS ALL GRAY AND

THE CHOCOLATE IS ALL GONE,

IT'S GOOD TO REMEMBER

I'VE GOT A FRIEND LIKE YOU.

Snuggle in God's arms.

Snuggle in God's arms. When you are hurting, when you feel lonely, left out, let Him cradle you, comfort you, reassure you of His all-sufficient power and love.

Kay Arthur

Love Bears all Things,
Believes all Things,
Hopes all Things,
Endures all Things.
Love Never Ends.
1 Corinthians 13:7,8

A Friend Is a Treasure

A friend is someone we turn to,

when our spirits need a lift.

A friend is someone we treasure,

for our friendship is a gift.

A friend is someone who fills our lives,

with beauty, joy, and grace.

And makes the world we live in

a better and happier place.

PLANT YOUR ♡ IN A GARDEN OF DREAMS

Friendship Garden

Friendship, like a garden,

starts out with little seeds.

Kindness, love, and laughter

that fulfills each other's needs.

With patience, understanding,

and tender loving care,

A friendship everlasting

the two of us will share.

SOMETIMES THE SKY SEEMS CLOUDY ALL DAY,

UNTIL A FRIEND COMES ALONG AND BRIGHTENS THE WAY.

I do not mean that no trials come.
They may come in abundance, but they cannot
penetrate into the sanctuary of the soul,
and we may dwell in perfect peace even in the
midst of life's fiercest storms.

———————————

Hannah Whitall Smith

RAIN DOWN YOUR LOVE

©Teresa Kogut

FRIENDS
HAVE A SPECIAL WAY
OF BRINGING JOY
TO EVERY DAY.

A good friend is someone

to do nothing much with

and find "nothing much" so much fun.

A good friend is talking and talking

about everything under the sun.

A good friend is someone who really is glad

when you've worked for and won a success,

Someone you don't have to be on your guard with

or be what you aren't to impress.

A good friend is so many wonderful someones

all mixed in a marvelous blend

Of memory making, of giving and taking,

a "now and forever" good friend.

Author Unknown

MAY YOUR SORROWS BE PATCHED AND YOUR JOYS BE QUILTED.

The little troubles and worries of life
may be as stumbling blocks in our way,
or we may make them stepping-stones
to a nobler character and to Heaven.
Troubles are often the tools by which God
fashions us for better things.

_____

Henry Ward Beecher

LORD,
HELP ME TO REMEMBER
THAT NOTHING IS GOING TO HAPPEN
TO ME TODAY THAT YOU AND I
TOGETHER CAN'T HANDLE.

All we
need is
LOVE

FRIENDSHIP BLOSSOMS
WITH KINDNESS

Don't Quit

When things go wrong, as they sometimes will,
When the road you're trudging seems all uphill,
When the funds are low, and the debts are high,
And you want to smile, but you have to sigh,
When care is pressing you down a bit,
Rest if you must, but don't you quit.

Life is queer with its twists and turns,
As every one of us sometimes learns,
And many a failure turns about,
When he might have won had he stuck it out;
Don't give up though the pace seems slow,
You may succeed with another blow.

Success is failure turned inside out,
The silver tint of the clouds of doubt,
And you never can tell how close you are,
It may be near when it seems so far.
So stick to the fight when you're hardest hit,
It's when things seem worse that you must not quit.

Author Unknown

don't quit

fight

Rest

19

FAITH WILL HELP US THROUGH

20

Today is the day
        to celebrate moments—
        to stop and feel the sunshine,
        to build your own rainbow.

Today is the day
        to celebrate chances,
        to make your own adventures.

Today is the day to live large and worry small
        to celebrate joy,
        to find the time to dream
        and to believe in miracles.

Author Unknown

No matter what you're going through,
if you really look for who He is, you will find Him
watching and caring for you.

Sandy Lynam Clough

May the road rise to meet you,
may the wind be always at your back.
May the sun shine warm upon your face,
the rains fall soft upon your fields.
And until we meet again, may God hold you
in the hollow of His hand.

An Irish Blessing

Friendship is a Sheltering Tree

A hug is a
handshake
from the heart.

Love isn't
Love until
you give
it away

There is something that we all share
An excellent talent that shows we care.
Everyone can do it big or small
Even people wide or tall.
I will share this talent just with you
It's a special hug from me to you.

Author Unknown

I said a prayer for you today and know God
must have heard. I felt the answer in my heart
although He spoke no word. I didn't ask for wealth
or fame, I knew you wouldn't mind. I asked Him
to send treasures of a far more lasting kind.
I asked that He'd be near you at the start of each
new day. To grant you health and blessings and
friends to share your way. I asked for happiness for
you in all things great and small. But it was for His
loving care I prayed the most of all.

Author Unknown

26

THE BEST
AND MOST BEAUTIFUL THINGS
IN THIS WORLD
CANNOT BE SEEN
OR EVEN TOUCHED. THEY MUST BE
FELT WITH THE HEART.

Tattered & Torn my old friends may be
but life's greatest
treasures they
remain
to me

© Teresa Kogut

27

God grant me the serenity
to accept the things I cannot change,
courage to change the things I can, and wisdom
to know the difference.

Reinhold Niehbuhr

Sometimes it is good for us to have troubles
and hardships, for they often call us
back to our own hearts . . . we should so root
ourselves in God that we do not need
to look for comfort anywhere else.

Thomas à Kempis

Come to me,
all you who are weary
and burdened,
and I will give you rest.

The Book of Matthew (NIV)

OLD☆TEDDIES

Our lives are full of supposes. Suppose this should happen, or suppose that should happen; what could we do; how could we bear it? But, if we are living in the high tower of the dwelling place of God, all these supposes will drop out of our lives. We shall be quiet from the fear of evil, for no threatenings of evil can penetrate into the high tower of God. Even when walking through the valley of the shadow of death, the psalmist could say, I will fear no evil; and, if we are dwelling in God, we can say so too.

Hannah Whitall Smith

God hath not promised
Skies always blue,
Flower strewn pathways
All our lives through.

God hath not promised
Sun without rain,
Joy without sorrow,
Peace without pain.

But God hath promised
Strength for the day,
Rest for the labor,
Light for the way,
Grace for the trials,
Help from above,
Unfailing sympathy,
Undying love.

Annie Johnson Flint

Nurture the Soul

Anything big enough

to occupy our minds

is big enough

to hang a prayer on.

George MacDonald

GOOD FRIENDS NURTURE THE SOUL AND CHEER THE HEART

When I finally reached a point where I wanted to quit, I found myself changed all at once. In my soul, which until that time was in distress, I suddenly felt a profound inward peace as if it were in its true place of rest. Ever since that time I have walked before God in simple faith, with humility and with love, and I apply myself diligently to do nothing and think nothing which might displease Him. I hope that when I have done what I can, He will do with me what He pleases.

Brother Lawrence

anything can happen

When God is involved,
anything can happen. Be open.
Stay that way. God has a beautiful way
of bringing good vibrations
out of broken chords.

Charles R. Swindoll

A HUG

IS THE SHORTEST DISTANCE

BETWEEN FRIENDS.

God of our life, there are days when the burdens we carry chafe our shoulders and weigh us down; when the road seems dreary and endless, the skies grey and threatening; when our lives have no music in them, and our hearts are lonely, and our souls have lost their courage. Flood the path with light, run our eyes to where the skies are full of promise; tune our hearts to brave music; give us the sense of comradeship with heroes and saints of every age; and so quicken our spirits that we may be able to encourage the souls of all who journey with us on the road of life, to Your honour and glory.

St. Augustine

Love thy Neighbor

OLD FRIEND

A true friend is distinguished
in the crisis of hazard and necessity; when
the gallantry of his aid may show the worth of his
soul and the loyalty of his heart.

———————

Ennius

WHEN TRUE FRIENDS MEET IN ADVERSE HOUR,

'TIS LIKE A SUNBEAM THROUGH A SHOWER;

A WATERY RAY AN INSTANT SEEN,

THE DARKLY CLOSING CLOUDS BETWEEN.

SIR WALTER SCOTT

41

Your Friendship
is like a warm
Sunny Day

LOVE BLOSSOMS WITH KINDNESS

The heart is a garden
That always has room
For the flowers of kindness
And friendship that blooms!
The beauty of friendship—
As every friend knows—
Is the loveliest blossom
In the heart where it grows!

OUR HELP IS IN THE NAME OF THE LORD,
THE MAKER OF HEAVEN AND EARTH.

THE BOOK OF PSALMS (NIV)

It's a good thing
to have all the props pulled out
from under us occasionally.
It gives us some sense
of what is rock under our feet,
and what is sand.

Madeleine L'Engle

GOD MADE US ALL

God is our refuge
and strength,
a very present help
in trouble.

The Book of Psalms

NEVER FEAR SHADOWS,

THEY SIMPLY MEAN

THERE'S A LIGHT SHINING

SOMEWHERE NEARBY.

FRIENDS TO THE END

No moving parts, no batteries.
No monthly payments and no fees.
Inflation proof, non-taxable,
In fact, it's quite relaxable.
It can't be stolen, won't pollute,
One size fits all, do not dilute.
It uses little energy,
But yields results enormously.
Relieves your tension and your stress,
Invigorates your happiness.
Combats depression, makes you beam,
And elevates your self-esteem!
Your circulation it corrects,
Without unpleasant side effects.
It is, I think, the perfect drug,
May I prescribe, my friend . . .
The Hug!
(and, of course, fully returnable)

Author Unknown